MW00411810

Published by Barbour Books, an imprint of Barbour Publishing, Inc.,
P.O. Box 719, Uhrichsville, Ohio 44683
www.barbourbooks.com

Member of the
Evangelical Christian
Publishers Association

Printed in China.

EVEN THOUGH
WE'RE FAR APART

SHANNON HILL

No one has ever seen God;
But if we love one another,
God lives in us and his love
Is made complete in us.

1 JOHN 4:12 NIV

A friend might well be reckoned
the masterpiece of nature.

RALPH WALDO EMERSON

Contents

My Friend,

I'm missing you today. You always seem to know the right words to make me see life with a fresh perspective. The challenge is applying all that we've learned together—even when we're far apart. I can get so lost in my own thoughts and an overwhelming sense of walking this road alone. But I know that God is with us both, and He is smiling, bridging the miles between our hearts.

WHEN WE'RE APART

Tom's mind was made up now.
He was gloomy and desperate.
He was a forsaken, friendless boy, he said;
nobody loved him.

FROM *The Adventures of Tom Sawyer*
BY MARK TWAIN

Mimicking the mischievous Tom Sawyer's melodramatic mood, I can sigh and fuss, fret and feel friendless. Where are you to bring in the sun and light up the room?

- I miss your support.

- I miss your listening ear.

- I miss your gentle companionship, reminding me that loneliness only lasts a moment but friendship an eternity.

I lie awake;
I am like a lonely bird on the housetop.

PSALM 102:7 NRSV

I miss the friend with whom I share my secrets. . .

Nothing makes us so lonely as our secrets.

PAUL TOURNIER

. . .and the one with whom I choose to break up the solitary moments with conversation and laughter.

Whoever is delighted in solitude is . . .a wild beast.

FRANCIS BACON

Days of absence, sad and dreary,
The one I love is far away.

JEAN-JACQUES ROUSSEAU

True friendship is like sound health,
the value of it is seldom known until it be lost.

CHARLES CALEB COLTON

These passions, like great winds, have blown me hither and thither, in a wayward course, over a deep ocean of anguish, reaching to the very verge of despair.

AUTHOR UNKNOWN

Be strong and take heart,
all you who hope in the LORD.

PSALM 31:24 NIV

The distance between us sometimes requires a strength and courage that challenges us to grow.

It's amazing how God stretches us. We face our aloneness. We do it apart, but together in spirit.

Courage is the price that life exacts for granting peace.
The soul that knows it not
knows no release from little things;
knows not the livid loneliness of fear.

AMELIA EARHART

*Sorrow is the rust of the soul
and activity will cleanse and brighten it.*

SAMUEL JOHNSON

My eyes are ever toward the LORD, for he will pluck my feet out of the net. Turn to me and be gracious to me, for I am lonely and afflicted. Relieve the troubles of my heart, and bring me out of my distress.

PSALM 25:15–17 NRSV

Things to Do When I Can't Spend Time with You

- Take up volunteer service
- Read a classic
- Write an "old-fashioned" paper letter
- Enjoy the outdoors
- Spend time with a child

When one door of happiness closes, another opens; but often we look so long at the closed door that we do not see the one which has opened for us.

Helen Keller

I know what it is to be in need, and I know what it is to have plenty. I have learned the secret of being content in any and every situation, whether well fed or hungry.

PHILIPPIANS 4:12–13 NIV

Though our communication

wanes at times of absence,

I'm aware of a strength that

emanates in the background.

CLAUDETTE RENNER

WHY YOU
ARE SPECIAL

"I shall depend on hearing from you very often, Eliza."
"*That* you certainly shall."
"And I have another favour to ask. Will you come and see me?"
"We shall often meet, I hope. . . ."

FROM *Pride and Prejudice*
BY JANE AUSTEN

When I think how we became friends or why we are friends still, I know that God knew we needed each other. As time has passed, we've taken different roads. Come what may, I know that our lives will be intertwined forever and that I will be a better person for knowing you and having you as my friend.

Each friend represents a world in us,
a world possibly not born until they arrive,
and it is only by this meeting that
a new world is born.

ANAIS NIN

Two may talk together under the same roof for many years, yet never really meet; and two others at first speech are old friends.

MARY CATHERWOOD

What is desirable in a person is loyalty.

PROVERBS 19:22 NRSV

A friend is one to whom one may pour out all the contents of one's heart, chaff and grain together, knowing that the gentlest of hands will take and sift it, keep what is worth keeping and with a breath of kindness blow the rest away.

ARABIAN PROVERB

I miss seeing your generous heart in action each day, knowing how you share your life and love with others.

Consciously or unconsciously,
every one of us does render some service or other.
If we cultivate the habit of doing this service deliberately,
our desire for service will steadily grow stronger,
and will make, not only our own happiness,
but that of the world at large.

GANDHI

Your friends define you, some say. Others may suggest they challenge you, confront you with candid honesty, or lead you down new trails. But friends like you accomplish all these things with grace and kindness, mercy and love.

Every heart that has beat strong and cheerfully
has left a hopeful impulse behind it in the world,
and bettered the tradition of mankind.

ROBERT LOUIS STEVENSON

The best portion of a good man's life—
his little, nameless, unremembered acts
of kindness and love.

WILLIAM WORDSWORTH

You have character, my friend. And a kind of class that is like a rare, distinct book. God knew what He was doing when He put the two of us together. This gift can't encompass the things I appreciate about you. Know that you enrich my life through your goodness, your spirit, your grace. . .your strength, confidence, and honesty.

I'm impressed with your courage.

In matter of style, swim with the current; in matters of principle, stand like a rock.

THOMAS JEFFERSON

I admire your confidence.

Self-confidence is the first requisite to great undertakings.

SAMUEL JOHNSON

And I appreciate your commitment to truth.

An honest answer is the sign of true friendship.

AUTHOR UNKNOWN

*Whoever loves his brother lives in the light,
and there is nothing in him to make him stumble.*

1 JOHN 2:10 NIV

Don't walk behind me,
I may not lead.
Don't walk in front of me,
I may not follow.
Just walk beside me
And be my friend.

ALBERT CAMUS

WHEN
WE'RE TOGETHER

"So all my plan is spoilt!" said Frodo.
"It is no good to try to escape you.
But I'm glad, Sam. I cannot tell you how glad.
Come along! It is plain that we were meant to go together."

FROM *The Fellowship of the Ring*
BY J. R. R. TOLKIEN

Chocolate and peanut butter. Puppies and little boys. Good books and rainy afternoons. Taxi cabs and New York City. Certain things in life were designed to go well together. When we get the chance to spend time with each other, our friendship ranks high among the stellar matches.

You will fill me with joy in your presence.

PSALM 16:11 NIV

Give me one friend, just one, who meets
The needs of all my varying moods.

ESTHER M. CLARK

*But I will see you again and you will rejoice,
and no one will take away your joy.*

JOHN 16:22 NIV

The sky seems to be a pure, a cooler blue,
the trees a deeper green. . .
The whole world is charged with the glory of God
and I feel fire and music. . .under my feet.

THOMAS MERTON

*I am beginning to learn that it is the sweet, simple
things of life which are the real ones after all.*

LAURA INGALLS WILDER

The very best thing about being apart is knowing that I will see you again and the anticipated joy of our meeting. Airports and driveways have taken on the unexpected role of red carpet host to our emotional reunions.

When we're together, the rewards of our friendship surface in strength. . .eclipsing any challenges of distance or time.

With you, I'll laugh until my sides ache.

I'll share my hurts and what makes me afraid.

With you, I'll watch the stars make
early evening appearances.

I'll explore the wonders of the universe
and what it really means to love someone.

Or I'll just enjoy the company of your silence.

When we're together. . .

All who would win joy must share it;
happiness was born a twin.

LORD BYRON

We're so fond of one another because
our ailments are the same.

JONATHAN SWIFT

There is an exquisite melody in every heart.
If we listen closely, we can hear each other's song.
A friend knows the song in your heart
and responds with beautiful harmony.

AUTHOR UNKNOWN

I am treating you as my friend
asking you share in my present minuses
in the hope I can ask you to share
in my future pluses.

KATHERINE MANSFIELD

A true friend may be rocked by the storms that shake our foundation, but that friend grabs a line and won't let go. You have been by my side, whether in body or spirit, through some of the most challenging moments of my life. You'll never know how much it means to me that you have been a shoulder to lean on.

Two are better than one;
because they have a good reward for their labour.
For if they fall, the one will lift up his fellow:
but woe to him that is alone when he falleth;
for he hath not another to help him up.

ECCLESIASTES 4:9–10 KJV

*Friendships multiply joys
and divide grief.*

THOMAS FULLER

*"Stay" is a charming word
in a friend's vocabulary.*

BRONSON ALCOTT

What binds us together is the prayer,
the promise and the lifting of each other's burdens,
the commitment we have made, and kept,
to be companions to each other on the road we share.
What binds us together is the laying down of our lives
for each other in a way that we cannot even explain.

ROBERT BENSON

WHAT I PRAY FOR YOU

My wish upon this shooting star is that your heart be happy.

FROM *Anne of Green Gables*
BY L. M. MONTGOMERY

Our time together passes by so quickly, then it's back to our homes, families, jobs, and simple geography. We return to the routine, and our memories fade amongst the bustle of every day. Yet, even across the distance, I have a gift to offer you. I give you my prayers.

My prayer for you, wherever you may be today, is for God's deepest blessing on your life and those you love. You are a friend beyond compare, and my thoughts of you will always contain a petition to our heavenly Father for His protection and guidance in your life.

I thank my God every time
I remember you.

PHILIPPIANS 1:3 NIV

Father, You alone know what lies before me this day,
grant that in every hour of it I may stay close to You.

JOHN BAILLIE

Blessed are the pure in heart,
for they will see God.

MATTHEW 5:8 NIV

May the blessings of light be upon you,
Light without and light within.
And in all your comings and goings,
May you ever have a kindly greeting
From them you meet along the road.

IRISH BLESSING

35

Dear God,

Bless my friend in this moment. . . .

- In the bleary-eyed, sleepy mornings

- In the rush-hour traffic

- In waiting rooms and post offices

- In cubicles or down grocery aisles

- In soccer carpools or at dance recitals

Allow Your child to walk in Your light and grace,
Discovering the ordinary of each day to be transformed
Into extraordinary moments by Your love.

I rejoice in life for its own sake.
Life is no brief candle to me.
It is a sort of splendid torch which
I have got hold of for a moment
and I want to make it burn as brightly as possible
before handing it on to future generations.

GEORGE BERNARD SHAW

Peace I leave with you;
my peace I give you.
I do not give to you as the world gives.
Do not let your hearts be troubled
and do not be afraid.

JOHN 14: 27 NIV

As I ask for God's blessing on your life and in each thing you do, I'll thank Him for our friendship, for it truly is a precious gift from heaven.

Blessed is the man who makes the LORD his trust.

PSALM 40:4 NIV

O Thou who has given us so much,
mercifully grant us one thing more—
a grateful heart.

GEORGE HERBERT

And did you get what you wanted
from this life even so?
I did.
And what did you want?
To call myself beloved, to feel myself
Beloved on the earth.

RAYMOND CARVER

*My dear friend, even though we are far apart,
separated by miles and the circumstances of life—
I'm thinking of you today.
I want you to know that you are loved—
and because of your life, I'm forever changed.*